James Monroe

BY BONNIE HINMAN

The Child's World®
childsworld.com

Published by The Child's World®
1980 Lookout Drive • Mankato, MN 56003-1705
800-599-READ • www.childsworld.com

Photographs ©: Maryann Groves/North Wind Picture
Archives, cover, 1; Picture History/Newscom, 4, 7, 11, 12; North
Wind Picture Archives, 8, 12, 15, 17; A. T. Stata/Library of
Congress, 18

ISBN 9781503816473
LCCN 2016945648

Printed in the United States of America
PAO2322

ABOUT THE AUTHOR

Bonnie Hinman has written more than 40 nonfiction books. She lives in Southwest Missouri with her husband, Bill, near her children and grandchildren. She graduated from Missouri State University in Springfield, Missouri.

Table of Contents

James Monroe has held more positions in public office than any other president to date.

CHAPTER ONE

The Era of Good Feelings

It was July 2, 1817. President James Monroe arrived in Boston, Massachusetts. A huge crowd welcomed him. More than 4,000 children were there. The boys wore blue coats. The girls wore white dresses. Everyone was excited to meet the president.

Monroe had been president for four months. He was from Virginia. He knew many people there.

But he wanted to meet more people. He decided to travel north.

Monroe began his trip on June 1, 1817. He wanted to travel simply. He planned to spend nights at public **inns**. But he realized his trip would not be quiet.

People heard he was traveling the country. They lined the roads to cheer for him. Town leaders welcomed him with speeches. Some days, Monroe gave five speeches himself.

Monroe's simple trip turned into a grand **tour**. People wanted to celebrate. The country had just won a war. **Politicians** had stopped their bitter fighting. People were making more money than ever before.

The trip took 15 weeks. Monroe acted like one of the people. In return, people showed how much they liked him. They rang church bells. They held parades.

Monroe stayed at many inns during his tour.

It was the beginning of a new time period. It was called the "**Era** of Good Feelings." People were happy during Monroe's trip. But the good feelings did not last.

Monroe served under George Washington during the Revolutionary War.

CHAPTER TWO

Before the Presidency

James Monroe was born on April 28, 1758. He was born in Virginia. His family was not rich. But they also were not poor. James's parents taught him to read and write. He started going to school at age 11. He walked 5 miles (8 km) to get to school.

James's parents died when he was a teen. His uncle paid for him to go to college. James went to the College of William and Mary. But he became a soldier before he finished school. He fought in the Revolutionary War. James joined the Virginia army.

Monroe studied law after the war. Thomas Jefferson helped teach him. Then Monroe's uncle gave Monroe an idea. He thought Monroe should work in politics.

Monroe first ran for office in 1782. He won a seat in the Virginia government.

Then Monroe got married in 1786. His wife's name was Elizabeth. They had three children. They had two daughters and one son. But their son died as a baby.

Years later, Monroe continued to work in politics. In 1790 he became a **senator** for Virginia. Then he became governor of Virginia in 1799.

In 1803, Monroe helped make a deal with France. He worked on it with Thomas Jefferson. It was called the Louisiana Purchase.

Elizabeth Monroe was influential during her husband's political career.

The United States bought 827,000 square miles (2,141,920 sq km) of land. The country almost doubled in size.

Monroe also was an important leader during the War of 1812. Then Monroe wanted to try one more job. He wanted to run for president.

Monroe was a member of the
Democratic-Republican political party.

CHAPTER THREE

A Founding Father

In 1816, Monroe became the fifth U.S. president. He is often called the last **founding father**. Monroe wanted to make the United States important.

In 1817, Spain owned Florida. Monroe wanted Florida to become a state. Many Seminole Indians lived in Florida. They were forced to give up their land. This made them angry. Sometimes they attacked homes in Georgia.

Monroe sent General Andrew Jackson to Florida. Jackson went to stop the fighting.

He took over a main city. Spain finally agreed to sell Florida. The United States bought it in 1819.

Later that year, the country entered a depression. Many people lost their jobs. This marked the end of the "Era of Good Feelings." Then the United States faced a bigger problem. The north and the south started to fight. States in the south wanted **slavery**. But many states in the north thought it was wrong. They wanted to get rid of it.

Monroe owned slaves. He was not against slavery. But he wanted the country to stay together. The country might break up if states continued to disagree.

In 1820 Monroe ran for a second **term**. He was liked by almost everyone. Nobody ran against him. This has only ever happened to one other president. Monroe won another term.

The disagreement with the Seminole Indians led to three conflicts with the United States.

The United States grew later that year. People wanted Missouri to become a state. But they fought about the new state.

Some leaders wanted to **ban** slavery in Missouri. Others wanted to allow it. Monroe said Congress needed to decide. But they could not agree.

Finally Congress had an answer. People also wanted Maine to become a state. Congress said Missouri and Maine would both become states. Missouri would allow slavery. Maine would not. This was called the Missouri Compromise.

The agreement also included another rule. Land from the Louisiana Purchase was still being divided. New states were being formed. Slavery would be banned in states north of Missouri. Monroe signed the bill on March 6, 1820.

Slaves were forced to work without getting paid.

The other states liked this plan. They did not want the country to break up. But the problem did not go away. Forty years later it would start a war.

The Monroe Doctrine is still essential to the
United States' work with other countries today.

CHAPTER FOUR

The Monroe Doctrine

In 1823, Monroe had a different problem. Russia, Prussia, and Austria were countries in Europe. They were working together. Monroe thought they might take over other countries. Many countries in South America were now free. They used to be owned by Spain. But the European countries wanted to take them back. Monroe wanted to stop them. He wanted to help other countries stay free.

On December 2, 1823, Monroe gave a speech. He spoke to the powerful European countries.

Monroe told them to leave North and South America alone. Then the United States would leave Europe alone. He did not want to make them angry. But he wanted them to understand his position.

This speech was later called the Monroe Doctrine. Europe listened. They stayed away.

In 1825 Monroe's term ended. He did not want to be president again. He moved back to Virginia.

Monroe was busy after he left office. He wrote a book about working with other countries. He also started writing a book about his life.

Monroe's wife Elizabeth was often sick. She died on September 23, 1830. Then Monroe became very ill. He died on July 4, 1831. The last of the founding fathers was gone.

Monroe did many important things as president. Six states were added when he was in office.

Monroe discussed what he would say to the European countries before giving his famous speech.

Goods from the new states were shipped east. People earned more money than ever before. Monroe made the United States strong. He stood up for countries in South America. **Future** presidents would use Monroe's speech. The good feelings did not last for Monroe. But he helped build a great nation.

1750

← **April 28, 1758** James Monroe is born in Westmoreland County, Virginia.

← **March 1776** Monroe enlists in the Third Virginia Infantry during the Revolutionary War.

← **May 6, 1782** Monroe is elected to the Virginia legislature.

← **December 1790** Monroe becomes a U.S. Senator from Virginia.

← **December 1799** Monroe is elected governor of Virginia.

← **April 1803** Monroe helps negotiate the Louisiana Purchase.

← **November 1816** Monroe is elected president of the United States.

← **June 1, 1817** Monroe begins a grand tour of the northeastern states.

← **March 3, 1820** Congress approves the Missouri Compromise.

← **November 1820** Monroe is elected president for a second term.

← **December 2, 1823** Monroe announces the Monroe Doctrine.

← **March 1825** Monroe retires to his home in Virginia.

← **July 4, 1831** Monroe dies in New York City.

1835

ban (BAN) To ban something is to forbid it. Some people wanted to ban slavery in Missouri.

era (IHR-uh) An era is a chunk of time where something important happens. During Monroe's presidency, Americans were in an "Era of Good Feelings."

founding father (FOUND-ing FAH-thur) A founding father was one of the people who helped form the U.S. government. Monroe was the last founding father of the United States.

future (FYOO-chur) The future is time that has not come yet. Future presidents used the Monroe Doctrine when working with other countries.

inns (INS) Inns are small hotels. Monroe stayed in inns during his long trip in 1817.

politicians (pol-uh-TISH-uhns) Politicians are people who seek or hold public office. Politicians were fighting for power before Monroe was elected president.

senator (SEN-uh-ter) A person who joins the senate, one of the governing bodies of the United States, is a senator. Monroe served as a senator for Virginia.

slavery (SLAY-vuh-ree) Slavery is when someone owns and controls another person. The north and south disagreed on slavery.

term (TURM) A term is a period of time an official serves in office. Monroe ran for a second presidential term in 1820.

tour (TOOR) A tour is traveling from place to place. Monroe took a big tour to the states in the north.

In the Library

Maestro, Betsy. *A More Perfect Union: The Story of Our Constitution.* New York: HarperCollins, 2008.

Sobel, Syl. *Presidential Elections and Other Cool Facts.* Hauppauge, New York: Barron's, 2012.

Stabler, David. *Kid Presidents: True Tales of Childhood from America's Presidents.* Philadelphia, PA: Quirk, 2014

On the Web

Visit our Web site for links about James Monroe: **childsworld.com/links**

Note to Parents, Teachers, and Librarians: We routinely verify our Web links to make sure they are safe and active sites. So encourage your readers to check them out!

INDEX